WORDS Springing Forth

VERONICA R. DEAL

Copyright © 2024 by Veronica Deal

All rights reserved.

No portion of this book may be reproduced in any form without written permission from the publisher or author, except as permitted by U.S. copyright law.

This publication is designed to provide accurate and authoritative information in regard to the subject matter covered. It is sold with the understanding that neither the author nor the publisher is engaged in rendering legal, investment, accounting or other professional services. While the publisher and author have used their best efforts in preparing this book, they make no representations or warranties with respect to the accuracy or completeness of the contents of this book and specifically disclaim any implied warranties of merchantability or fitness for a particular purpose. No warranty may be created or extended by sales representatives or written sales materials. The advice and strategies contained herein may not be suitable for your situation. You should consult with a professional when appropriate. Neither the publisher nor the author shall be liable for any loss of profit or any other commercial damages, including but not limited to special, incidental, consequential, personal, or other damages.

Acknowledgments

I would like to say thank you to my Lord and Savior, Jesus Christ, for without him I could do nothing. I would also like to thank my husband of thirty-eight years, Gary Deal, for pushing me and supporting me and telling me I can do this, for seeing the vision when I lost the vision, and for making me believe that this and other books can become reality. Thank you, Gary. To my sons, Darius Deal and Germany Deal, my grandkids, Eric, Marianna and DJ; my family, who I love dearly; and my pastor and his first lady, for praying for me, letting me read my poems and poetry at different functions, inspiring me to do better, to be better. Thank you all!

Title derived from Bible scripture found in the book of Isaiah.

Behold I will do a new thing;

now it shall spring forth;

shall ye not know it?

I will even make a way in the wilderness.

—Isaiah 43:19

All the Glory

All the glory goes to him alone,

For all the love that he has shown,

For giving me skills to be able to write,

For putting words in my head, both day and night.

When I read to people the words God gave me,

It never ceases to amaze me,

How all the words fit together.

May these words last forever!

As I end this poem,

I repeat this phrase:

All the glory belongs to God,

And I'll say it for the rest of my days!

OCTOBER 16, 2017

Dreams of a Little Girl

Sometimes in life, as little girls we dream

That we could have the whole world,

But then the more we grow,

The more we know that this is not always so.

Bits and pieces here and there

Let us know that life is not always fair.

But there is still hope, and we can dream of happiness

And peace in Jesus, our king,

For when we know who he is, we can have it all,

Because he lives.

So dream, little girls;

With nurture, love, and care,

You can have the world.

August 29, 2016

Hot Summer Day

Oh, do you remember

Those hot summer days?

If you've grown older now,

It might be a haze.

Let me remind you

Of what we used to do:

On a hot summer day,

The family has a barbecue,

With chicken and sausage,

And wieners on the grill,

Smell the awesome smoke,

Mmmmhh, get your fill.

The ladies bring dishes

Of salads of all kinds.

Oh no, at this barbecue

There is no wine;

We eat and grub

On all that's good and hot,

Then wash it all down

With soda pop.

This is a good time

To sit laugh and chat

About old times

We just can't get back.

Now yes, it's hot outside,

A hot summer day,

The best of the best

For kids to run and play.

— ❦ —

Sᴇᴘᴛᴇᴍʙᴇʀ 6, 2016

My COGIC Church

This is the Church of God in Christ,

Founded by Bishop Mason long ago in my life.

I grew up in it with no choice of my own;

We were in it more than at home.

Filled with the Holy Ghost at the age of twelve,

I didn't know why then, but only time would tell.

Mama made us go to church all the time;

I didn't understand, felt as though my life was not mine.

But as I grew older over the years,

I would learn Christ through many tears.

I learned for myself how to call on God;

He heard my prayers and fixed things I could not solve.

I've seen many people who claimed to be saints,

But their version and Christ's version were in my complaint.

I've seen pastors from different dominations,

But if their heart wasn't right, there would be condemnation.

From this church to that church and many all around,

I love my COGIC church, I'm rooted and ground.

SEPTEMBER 6, 2016

A Time and a Season

There's a time to laugh and a time to cry,

In your life there's a time for goodbye.

Bye to the old ways, hello to the new,

Be led by the Holy Spirit, he'll tell you what to do,

You might pray for release for one thing or another,

But only God Almighty knows our struggle.

There's a time to fight and a time to run;

Only you know when this has begun.

You'll have ups and you'll have downs,

But this I know: God is always around.

There's a time to pray and a time to fast;

If you don't, then you won't last.

I write this poem for one very reason:

To let you know today I'm in my season!

SEPTEMBER 6, 2016

Anticipation

I rise early in the morning with a prayer that is burning:

"Thank you, God, for waking me up,"

I say this before my morning cup.

All the things in store for today,

I know Jesus will lead the way.

I'm so excited about what's ahead

I toss and turn all night in bed!

It's the holy convocation that's going on now,

We've got work to do, God's gonna give us a crown!

With my first lady as the speaker tonight,

With the words in her heart, I know she'll be out of sight.

In attendance tonight will be bishops and superintendents and guests,

But for our Lord and Savior, we will do our best.

On the closing night, Thursday, it is,

This will go down in history and through the years.

Yes, anticipation for what's coming tonight!

Yes, at Greater Holmes Street Church of God in Christ!

SEPTEMBER 7, 2016

Amazing God

What can I say when I speak of my God?

Oh, that he's amazing and quick as a lightning rod!

He'll answer your prayers in such a way,

Change your life in a day.

Just when you think that things are over,

God shows up and treat you better than a brother.

Oh, what an amazing God that we serve!

No one is like him in the whole world.

I'll put my trust in him, because others will fail,

I'm on the right path, I don't want to go to hell.

I'll lift up my hands in praise to thee.

In God's amazing arms is right where I want to be.

SEPTEMBER 8, 2016

The Woman with the Need Meets the Woman with No Faith

"Speak, Lord, speak," I could hear the woman say

As she begins to kneel down and pray.

When she came to the church, she had a need in mind,

She was looking for deliverance on holy ground.

Oh, but do you know there was a mistake that she made?

She kneeled beside a woman that had no faith.

"How could you tell," you say, "that the woman had no faith?"

Because she only came because they were giving away free plates.

So as the woman with the need began to pray,

The woman with no faith began to say,

"Girl, I don't know what you praying fo'!

I already know how this gon' go.

You pray for this and you pray for that,

Girl, God don't never have my back."

So the woman with the need looked at the woman with no faith,

And she said, "Close your eyes, shut your mouth, and begin to pray."

As the woman with the need took the hand of the woman with no faith,

Oh my god, the building began to shake—the Holy Ghost was here.

The holy ghost is here!

"Woman, release all your fears,

Pray for one another and let God have his way."

The woman with the need could have gotten up and moved

And left the woman with no faith to keep walking in the same old shoes.

So the moral of this story is:

Care for one another,

Not just your blood sister or brother.

SEPTEMBER 18, 2016

Choices

As we wake in the morning,

There are choices being made.

One of them is

That you get out of bed.

We should say, "Thank you,"

To God above,

For showing us kindness, grace, and love.

From this day ahead,

I know that I'll pray that I am led,

By the Holy Spirit,

To touch a life today.

I want to be pleasing to God in every way.

Do I speak of his goodness,

Or do I hold my tongue?

Lead me, Holy Spirit, so I don't go wrong.

Who am I to tell the people

That God is on his way?

There are choices to be made,

And that's heaven or hell.

I'm telling you now,

My soul is not for sale.

As I make the choice in my life today,

I choose to live for God;

I don't want it any other way!

September 27, 2016

Why?

Why aren't things ever like they seem?

You think things are one way,

But it's just a dream.

When you wake,

It's all the same.

You try to do better

But get the blame.

Packing up your stuff because you got to move,

If you try to reason,

then you're giving attitude.

Why, Lord, why aren't things ever like they seem?

When I wake up, I realize,

It was all a dream.

I dreamed of a life of security,

But man, of course, it keeps tricking me.

Why, Lord, why do I fall for his lies?

When will I wake up and realize

This life is mine?

My hopes and dreams, my hopes and dreams.

Why, Lord, why?

Why aren't things as they seem?

I dreamed of a life

Where I'd own a home one day,

But the older I get,

The further and further it seems to be away.

But now I'm awake and with faith I can see

One day my dreams can be reality.

Even though in my life I ask God why,

I am determined to live

And join him in the sky.

Why, Lord, why?

Why do I not see

That you're just working things out for me?

Not by my strength and not by my might.

I'll turn this over to Jesus,

This is not my fight.

Why? Part 2

As the question was answered later on this day,

A door was opened and God made a way.

The thing that I asked for was the thing that God did.

Now I'm happy and my heart is filled with gratitude and peace.

I believe this is God's will.

So for this reason, I won't ask God why.

I'll just keep thanking him by and by.

September 27, 2016

From Failure to Victory

When your head's against the wall

And you can't see anything at all,

Truth and faith will see you through,

Yes, my God really loves you.

Though trials and tests

May come your way.

It all must finish

At the end of the day.

So have some patience,

Slow your roll,

Satan's trying to hinder you

From your goal.

From failure to victory,

You'll say one day,

When you tell your story

Along the way:

"I started with my head

Against the wall,

But my God

Saw me through it all."

— ※ —

April 21, 2017

Family

From the beginning we have a dad and a mom.

Some of us cling to them, some of us run.

You may have a bro, you may have a sis.

Some of us are blessed more than we wish.

Back to my mama and daddy too.

That's my family, yeah, that's my crew.

We eat together, laugh, and pray.

Some of us go, some of us stay.

Even from a distance we call on the phone.

I never feel as though I am alone.

April 24, 2017

The Glory

All the glory belongs to God,

If you think you deserve it, you are fraud,

For God's Word tells us that he is just;

If you believe this, then you have to trust

That God's Word is real and true,

The trials and tests that he takes you through

Are for his glory and not for you.

If you are proud and very vain,

Then you won't accomplish, not a one single thing.

For all the glory belongs to God.

If you want it for yourself, then you will fall.

What is this glory?

Do you understand?

It is for God and not for man.

With our hands lifted and our mouth filled with praise,

Give God the glory

All your days.

April 27, 2017

Don't Let Things Consume You

What are the things you do the most?

On a daily basis, come on, don't boast.

From morning to night and in between,

Let's make a list of what this means.

When you rise in the morning

And go on your way,

Do you remember to thank God

And go for your day?

Sing a little song or even pray?

Come on now, you're making a list;

This is for real and not just a wish.

Is it Facebook, TV, or radio too?

Please don't let things consume you!

For you will look and realize one day

That all your time's wasted on things falling away.

Now that you examined your list today,

If you don't like it, throw it away.

You can make a new list, it's okay.

At the top and bottom too,

List the things that won't consume you.

April 27, 2017

It's the Night before Mother's Day

It was the night before Mother's Day,

And all through the house not a person was stirring, not even a mouse.

Mothers were dreaming of a good day to come.

Those that were holy were praying for everyone.

Flowers and balloons and chocolates too.

Sweet, sweet mothers, these are for you.

It was the night before Mother's Day and all through the house,

Gifts were being hidden by children and the spouse.

Some gifts were great, and some were small;

Some mothers knew they would get no gifts at all.

Oh, but how sweet and kind mothers are!

They know we love them from here, near and far.

As I come to a close, I want to say a special thanks

To our own first lady, who is such a sweet saint.

To you and all those who are mothers,

Keep on doing *you* like no other.

With our arms and hearts open so wide,

It makes it all worth it to see your great big smile.

Happy Mother's Day!

May 13, 2017

To My Mother

Mother's Day poem by Gary Deal

To my mother, I'd like to say,

I am missing you this Mother's Day.

As I think of many things,

I could only remember them in my dreams.

Finally, one day we will meet—

Oh, what a wonderful day it will be!

When we are laughing, talking,

With no cares of the day,

Sharing a dance, having it my way.

I love and miss you, Mom,

On this Mother's Day!

May 12, 2017

Chat with My Mama

My mom called on the phone—

Oh, what a joy, we talked on the phone!

How I did enjoy!

We caught up on all the things going on,

I just didn't like that it was over phone.

I miss talking to my mom!

One-on-one, we would talk until midnight

Or until we were done.

She told me about her church,

I told her about mine.

We talked about how in God we had a good time.

She mentioned sister Betty in this conversation,

And also how Pastor Wo was getting them ready

To travel the world in God's name,

Showing them how to ride a plane.

She told me all the goodness that God is doing for her.

My mama deserves more,

Even mink and fur.

I'm glad she's getting her roses while she's yet alive.

She will receive more, double, triple, and multiplied.

May 29, 2017

Love Is Pain

Love and pain go hand in hand,

It's all about love between you and your man.

Some days are good, some are bad.

The way love does you is kind of sad.

You must figure out if you want to stay.

Don't be hasty and run away.

What God has joined together, let no man divide.

If it's true and real, the love won't hide.

I am your woman, you are my man,

Let's get this marriage together, it's part of God's plan.

After thirty-four years of this love and pain,

We just can't expect things to stay the same.

I have gray hair here, you have it there,

If God blesses us, we'll have it everywhere.

Remember my dream that I would often share,

Sitting on my porch, rocking my chair.

With Eric and Marianna and our other grandchildren visiting us

For summers throughout the years.

So you see, with some love, there may be pain,

But with work and effort it's all worth the gain.

As anniversaries come and anniversaries go,

Cherish your love, don't let it walk out the door.

When he say go, you stay.

Remember, breathe, take time to pray.

He calls you bae, you call him hun,

Fast together, pray together, stay united as one.

Where there's love, there's pain,

Yet victory can be won.

June 13, 2017

Workflo'

There's this girl at work, y'all, she's a trip.

All the guys look at her because she got thick hips.

She put forward the effort, she makes beautiful cakes,

But she's often goofin' off throughout the day.

Don't get me wrong, she's a good friend to me,

I'm just telling you how things usually be.

When the manager tells her, "Hey, do this,"

She just looks at him and says, "Man, quit."

Even his manager is sneaky and shy,

Always avoiding her so he can get by.

Ya'll, she's loud, and ghetto too,

I'm not talking about her, just saying what she do.

I never talk about her behind her back,

I only discuss things that are facts.

I try to tell her, ""Hey, you need to do this,"

She just rolls her eyes at me, as a kind of dismiss.

We get along good, we're from the same state.

We have arguments and very common debates.

Now back to my title, which is called "Workflo',"

There's only three of us, ya'll, we go for what we know.

June 13, 2017

Can You Hear Me

I'm crying, Lord, can you hear me?

I'm hurting, Lord, can you feel me?

It's been a long time,

I've been calling, I've been seeking,

I've been dreaming, but still no answer.

Can you hear me? Can you feel me? Do you see me?

I've been waiting and hoping and anticipating,

Still no answer, yet I'm wating.

They say faith the size of a mustard seed,

I've been crying and hurting, dreaming and waiting,

But all I'm getting is no good deeds.

Can you hear me, Lord?

Do you feel me? Do you see me?

I won't ask where you are, because I know you are here,

But when I need you, you don't feel near.

Can you hear me?

Words Springing Forth

Feel me?

See me?

I am determined, and my mind is made up,

I'm trusting and believing you are making me tough.

I know you have the power and you are allowing me to go through.

Yes, you see me, feel me, and will bring me out.

Nobody but you!

August 26, 2017

Time

As we go through life day in and day out,

Some are blessed to make it through the night.

Some are drifters, not knowing how to live,

Lost and confused, overwhelmed with bills.

Some live happily and in a merry bliss,

Choosing not to see what life really is.

Some are wealthy, some are poor,

But it doesn't really matter when death is at your door,

Use this time wisely, give your life to Christ,

Follow him, serve him, give him your whole heart,

Because tomorrow's not promised,

It's time to make your mark.

Some people spend this life angry and mad,

If you don't ask for forgiveness,

This is gonna end bad.

Use this life wisely,

Live, laugh, and love;

They are all gifts from above.

Do what you can for others every day that you are here,

The day, the time for rapture,

Is drawing near!

— ❦ —

August 26, 2017

It's Time to Look Up Now

You've been down long enough,

Lift up your heads!

O ye gates and the King of Glory shall come in,

And God will bring you up and out of the pit.

He will bring you from failure to victory,

From weariness to joy,

From bondage to freedom.

He works great miracles, you won't believe it.

Yes, it was hard,

Yes, it was trying,

Yes, it hurt,

Yes, they left,

Yes, you cried,

Yes, you felt pain,

But it was never in vain.

Look up now, it's a new day.

Great things will happen, they are already on the way!

Decree it, declare it, receive it now:

Joy is yours,

Peace is yours,

Victory is yours,

Happiness is yours.

You've been put on notice,

Yes, you've been served.

Don't believe me, believe God,

Believe you can have these things.

For him nothing's too hard.

Thanksgiving Day

As I planned month by month, day by day,

To take a trip where my family stays,

On bus or car, I was planning to go,

I was so excited I couldn't stand it no more.

He was okay, but I was excited,

I guess I should've known, he didn't care about it.

I planned what I was going to wear,

Jogging pants and tennis shoes the entire day.

Now Sunday, Monday, Tuesday,

I was all set to go,

But then on Wednesday, it was for sure,

All my excitement was out the door.

I was so mad, but I played so cool,

Because the devil could use me and play me for a fool.

As I watched on Facebook,

All my family was there.

Hello, I'm missing, does anyone care?

I long for the day when my burdens and problems

Gonna have to take flight,

I'm going to use these wings God gave me.

One day, freedom, freedom, is what I'll be able to say.

See me, feel me, hear me roar,

There's something knocking at the door.

So I cooked food here for his family today

Because that is the "Christian" way.

Regardless of all the ways you feel,

People must know that Jesus is real.

Someone might ask, "What are you thankful for?"

There are so many answers if I say one, there will be more.

But the best thing I can truly say,

God allowed me to live this Thanksgiving Day!

A Woman's Heart

My heart throbs, aches, beats for life and all it has for me,

Bound, I say, bound by things I cannot see,

Things stopping me, holding me, but yet driving me to be free.

Places I wanna go, things I wanna see,

At my present time and state, it's not meant to be.

If I were alone, it would be a different story,

There would be no place I wouldn't go, things I wouldn't discover.

My heart throbs, aches, and beats and longs to be free!

Through my love of God, this will all come true,

Then my heart will smile and he will say,

"Yes, my child, for you!"

October 30, 2017

Struggles

As a mother I struggle!

As a wife I struggle!

As a Christian I struggle!

And as a human I struggle!

Day by day, as God wakes me out of bed,

I begin to struggle and then dread,

Because I know there's a voice waiting to put me down and say,

"You ain't never gonna be nothing, now have a good day."

I struggle to understand why there's so much hurt and pain,

Seems like everyone takes and there's nothing left to gain

Even on my job I struggle for promotion,

But no one can see my efforts through all the commotion.

I struggle to get through working there day by day,

I know if I don't work, I won't get paid.

I struggle as a mother to love and give advice,

But I have a soft, gentle spirit, and for young men that won't suffice.

I struggle as a wife of who this man wants me to be,

His dreams and fantasies of an ideal wife, it's just not me.

For inside of me there is a struggle to live free and be at peace,

But then my flesh reminds me that my struggle is a reality!

October 30, 2017

Lord, Bless Our Grandchildren

"Lord, bless our grandchildren," is our prayer today

Some of us can't see them because they live far away

Thank you, Lord, for telephones and Facebook too

Our only means of communication, those are tools we use

For because of our sons and daughters, we are given such great gifts

"Lord, bless my grandchildren," is my prayer and wish

Eric and Marianna, I'm missing y'all so much

Lord, bless my grandchildren, with your special touch

As the years go by, y'all are getting so big

To hug, kiss, and hold y'all is one thing I wish

I'm trying to be patient and let things work out

Don't want them to forget about us or have any doubts

That you are loved and truly missed

God, Lord, Jesus, bless our grandchildren

That is my wish

November 8, 2017

Wednesday

Today is Wednesday, and you, Lord, woke me up

Bless me this day, Lord, and fill my cup

With all you have for me on this rainy day

On this Wednesday, Lord, have your way

Thank you for your goodness and mercy too

I don't know what to do without you

Lord, you let me make it to the middle of the week

Thank God it's Wednesday, help me stay humble and meek

For I know this day you woke me, you had me on your mind

That's what kind of God you are, loving and kind

November 8, 2017

So It's Your Birthday

So today you're forty-nine,

I bet you think you're sexy and fine!

I don't mind the way you look,

'Cause you don't mind the things I cook.

Oh, yesterday you were forty-eight!

If you're trying to recapture, oops, you're too late!

For that day is in the past, now begin to have a blast!

So, Gary Deal, you celebrate,

It's only 7:00 p.m., it's not too late'

As gray hair comes in odd places,

Just ignore the look on our faces.

LOL!

As the young people write,

We learn what it means

Laugh out loud, it's all right!

DECEMBER 14, 2017

Can We Talk?

Mother, I'm trying to be all that you imagined me to be,

from the beginning, even in the womb,

God's been working miracles for me,

like he did with the tomb.

I know you're always standing there

with your arms open wide,

even when I come to you

with tears in my eyes.

You wrap your arms around me

and show me motherly love,

even thou my personality makes you wanna kick me to the curb.

But if you search your history, you will soon discover,

I act like you and you like your mother.

I am your daughter, and the words I speak are true—

look at me, Mother, I've blossomed and grown

and have kids and a husband of my own.

I know you want what's best for me deep down in your heart,

love me, love him, that's how you play that card.

Whatever's not right or good enough for you,

let God handle it, he's the man, he's the clue,

the glue that binds us all together, for now and eternity,

and yes, ever and ever, he's God, let him do what he do!

Thanks for the talk, Mother!

He Is

He is a man of standards,

Who preaches holiness or hell.

If you are in his presence,

You can tell.

Sixty-eight years in the ministry,

Oh, what a story to hear!

Moving from different locations

And having amazing careers,

For he is superintendent,

The awesome man of the hour,

Preaching holiness or hell

With authority and power!

As I try to hold back my tears,

Let me tell you who he is.

He is a preacher, a teacher,

And a mentor of mine;

All this just didn't happen,

But over years and time.

For you are loved by many,

And you love them back,

We appreciate you, Superintendent,

We'll always have you back!

October 12, 2018

Crime Today

As we look at the crime happening in 2016,

You say to yourself, Where's the hope and the dreams?

Prayer warriors, intercessors, pray!

The Bible did tell us this would happen one day.

Women with women, men with men,

Oh my god, the world is full of sin!

Man wants to conform to all the things today,

Some are running from the holy way.

Bishops, superintendents, and pastors too,

Please come up with a plan on what else we can do.

We are not just calling on all dignitaries, no sir,

Also them, him, me, and her,

To stand up and do all God has said:

Feed God's people his holy Word.

People are dying, hopeless, and without a cause,

Come on, Christians, saints, let's destroy these walls!

Crime is happening, whether you believe it or not,

Over here, over there, yes, every spot!

— ⚘ —

Made in the USA
Columbia, SC
20 April 2024